God's Word Works, No Matter How U Work It!

Joyce S. Daniels

Kindle Direct Publishing

United States of America

To request permissions, contact the publisher at joycedaniels67@gmail.com.

Paperback: 9798590229154

First paperback edition January 2021.

Edited by MieKayla L. Singleton

Cover art by Joyce S. Daniels

Layout by Joyce S. Daniels

Printed by Kindle Direct Publishing, in the United States of America.

First printing, 2021.

Publisher Email

joycedaniels67@gmail.com

Table of Contents

Dedication

This book is dedicated to the precious memories of Sherman Maurice Daniels, my beloved uncle, for his ultimate sacrifice for me.

In memory of Mary Ellen Daniels, my beloved grandma, who I was blessed to have all of my life. She lived a long 94 years of life until she went home to be with the Lord in April of 2020.

To Claudette Daniels, my wonderful mom, who fought a tough grief battle after my grandmother's passing. She is still standing and has always been there for me, her one and only. Love you, Mom.

Rhonda Howell, who was, and still is, one of my best friends. She was very sensitive to my being in danger.

And lastly, to the entire Daniels Family. You all have always been there to support me and encourage me. Love you all forever.

Preface

I hope that as you read my testimony of how my life experiences became a road map of confirmation of the power and truth of God's Word, you recognize that your own life experiences can do the same for you as well. May you discover for the first time, if not already, that God's Word is indeed active, alive, powerful, and sharper than a two-edged sword and a must to live by.

As you journey through my story, may you have an "aha" moment of your own. May you realize how your words have contributed to the life you are living. May you be reminded that your words create, frame, and shape your life and world. I hope that by the conclusion of this book, you understand that you can have whatsoever you say, whether that be "good" or "evil." Happy reading!

Chapter 1

The Power of the Tongue

While attending a conference in December of 2015, I received a prophetic word that confirmed that I needed to share my testimony. I began asking the Holy Spirit what part of my testimony He wanted me to reveal and how He wanted me to reveal it. I asked, "Is it from the perspective of me not knowing Him intimately, yet practicing His ways of doing things?" For instance, it was during this time that I realized that I had the power of influence. While working at a beauty supply store in Beltway Plaza Mall in 1985, I began crushing on a young man who worked as a security guard. He was 6'2" tall, slim, and fine to me. However, I had no idea how he'd feel about me. After all, I was a beautiful young lady who was 5'8" tall and plus-sized. I hadn't dated much. However, I remained silently hopeful for a while. Then, my bestie came up with the brilliant idea of playing Matchmaker, as she was willing to let him know that she knew someone who was interested in him. To my surprise, he revealed that he already knew that I was his secret admirer. When she asked how he knew, he replied that he saw how I looked at him. He then admitted that he thought I was attractive but that he had never dated a plus-sized young lady before. However, he stated that we could be friends, and he gave her his number to give to me. Being considerate of my feelings, my bestie didn't share this information with me right away. But when she finally did, I was hurt…but for only a minute. See, the confidence within me rang out loudly. With that being said, I decided to go ahead and take his number, intending to call him. I said to myself, "He would like me so much that he'd want to marry me." Well, after six months of being just friends and getting to know each other, he became so intrigued by me that he wanted to marry me. At that moment, I had a revelation of who I was: a nice, loving, heartfelt, caring young lady. Somewhere and somehow within me, I came to understand and know the power of my words.

It wasn't until I began to study the Word of God that I truly started to become aware of the power that lies within my tongue. Many scriptural pieces of evidence talk about having power over the words that you speak. These evidences can be found in Proverbs, Mark, Genesis, and Romans, and they can all be located in the King James Version. Proverbs 18:21-22 says that "death and life are in the power of the tongue: and they that love it shall eat the fruit thereof." Mark 11:22 says that "I have whatsoever I say." Genesis 1:26-28 says, via God, that "we've been created in His image and after His likeness." This particular verse means that we are speaking spirits just as God is a spirit. And in reference to Abraham in Romans 4:17, it says that "he called those things that be not as though they were." That is exactly what I had done, which allowed me to achieve the "God kind of results." Specifically, I declared that the young man would like me and that he would also want to marry me. That's exactly what happened, as I ended up touching a place in his heart within the first two months of our friendship. In addition, he not only wanted to date me the "right" way, but he also wanted to relocate states in order to get away from the fast life in D.C. and discover what he really wanted to do with his life. When he came clean to me about his plans of relocating, I was devastated. It literally felt like my plans to win him over were all for nothing and a waste of time. But perhaps I had that thought a moment too soon. See, what I didn't know is that he wanted to make these changes because of me and the impact that I had on him and his life.

In 1986, he moved away at the end of January. We corresponded through letters and some phone calls. In April, I decided to visit a friend in college, and I had the idea that he should come along with me. After that weekend, he was determined to come back home with the sole purpose of being with me, which is just what he did. However, by mid-June, he revealed that he went ahead and signed up for the U.S. Army. I couldn't help but think, "Oh, here we go again. I've just gotten what I declared. Now, he's off to the military? Are you kidding me??" Unbeknownst to me, yet again, this was another decision to better himself for us in order to create a long-term life together. Suddenly, everything clicked as I remembered my declarations. Specifically, I stated that "he would like me so much that he would want to marry me." Within six months, that's precisely what ended up happening.

There truly is power in the tongue. Whether it speaks good or evil, words come to life. Being aware of and residing in the Kingdom of God, I make every effort to be very careful with my words. After all, it is my duty as a child of God to be like Him. As a matter of fact, I should be so like him that even unbelievers end up seeing Him when they come in contact with me. Matthew 5:48 makes this point very clear by saying, "Be ye therefore perfect, even as your Father which is in heaven is perfect." Everything that the Lord speaks comes to pass! John 6:63 also references the power of the tongue. It says, "My words are life and spirit." In that verse alone, God reminds us of the power of the spoken Word. In like manner, to avoid negative life results, we too must speak life-filled words. Another way to prevent such results is by guarding our hearts in the best way possible. Proverbs 4:23 drives this point home by saying, "Keep your heart with all diligence, For out of it spring the issues of life."

I finally came to the realization that God was drawing me for years. It was He who called me out of the world into His marvelous light. It was He who granted me the strength to live Holy unto Him. It was He who gave me the desire to please Him above my flesh because of the great love I have for Him. In Psalm 37:4, God says, "Delight thyself also in the LORD; and he shall give thee the desires of thine heart."

Chapter 2

The Beginning of My Walk With Christ

In 1991, I was a member of the Young Adult Choir. I distinctively remember our choir director bringing us together with other churches that he directed. By doing this, my choir and I would find many ways to fellowship with other amazing church choirs. There would be services held that would allow us to sing, pray, and preach the gospel to each other. I actually had the great privilege of preaching a sermon at one of the services. The message was entitled "Satan Don't Live Here Anymore." You may recall a popular 70s soul and R&B group called Rose Royce. In 1978, they released one of their hit songs entitled "Love Don't Live Here Anymore." In this case, I replaced the word "Love" with "Satan" to state my view. Before I knew it, a hunger and a thirst had begun to grow on the inside of me to know God more. But this was after I dismissed Satan by denouncing and evicting him from my life.

While visiting a coworker's church one Sunday, I received a prophetic word from Jeremiah 29:11. This Scripture says, "For I know the thoughts that I think toward you, saith the LORD, thoughts of peace, and not of evil, to give you an expected end." With this Word, the fire began burning deep within me. At that moment, an even greater quest for Abba came. It seemed that every time I turned around, God kept making it clear that He wanted more from me and more of me. I'd given up so much for Him and His Gospel that I wasn't quite sure what more I could give Him. However, I did as He commanded and sought out how I could give Him more and in what ways I could give Him more.

Chapter 3

Bible College Days

While riding past the National Church of God in 2001, I noticed their National Bible College and Seminary sign. Instantly, I thought to find out what the requirements were to attend the school. I also figured, "Well, I'll apply, and if I get in, I'll know that this is part of the 'more' you want from me." Ironically enough, my former pastor had suggested that I go to Wesley Theological Seminary. At the time, I did not have an undergrad degree. In reality, that would've been problematic because having an undergrad degree was one of the prerequisites to attend Wesley. I went into NBC&S that day and received all the information I needed. From there, I began the process of enrollment. At the time, I was pursuing a double bachelor's degree in Evangelism and Christian Counseling. More than anything, I wanted to discover more of why God put me here on this earth, and I wanted to please Him. It only took me a little while to realize that enrolling in the NBC&S was one of the best decisions of my life. I would meet great instructors, professors, classmates, and the like. For me, it felt so awesome to be around people of like precious faith.

At NBC&S, our devotion times were awesome because we experienced and encountered God in many new and different ways. In addition, our devotion times ignited an even more burning desire within me to see the Word of God active in my generation. At this point, I was a member of a United Methodist Church. While the church preached the Word of God, it didn't *teach* about applying the Word of God. As one of my biggest desires, I really wanted to see God's Word lived out daily.

The Word speaks of being a child of God and also believing the power that He's equipped you with. After all, it can be easy to doubt the power of God that resides in you. But as children of God, we can't do that. Scriptural evidence can be found in the books of Matthew and Mark. Matthew 28:18-20 makes this clear by saying, "And Jesus came and spake unto them saying, "All power is given unto me in heaven and in the earth; Go ye therefore, into all of the world/nations, baptizing them in the name of the Father, Son, and Holy Spirit. Teaching them to observe to do all things whatsoever I have commanded you: and lo, I am with you alway[s], even unto the end of the world." Also, Mark 16:17 makes this even more clear by saying, "And these signs shall follow them that believe: in my name they shall cast out Devils: they shall speak with new tongues. They shall take up serpents and if they drink any deadly thing, it shall not hurt them; they shall recover." In this particular Scripture, God said, "These signs shall follow them that believe, they shall lay hands on the sick and the sick shall recover." I didn't see this happening and I wondered why. As I read, studied, and meditated on the Word, I realized what was missing. We had what the Scripture said: "having a form of godliness." However, we were "denying the power thereof." Upon educating myself on what was missing, I realized that I no longer wanted to do the bare minimum by just attending church; I wanted to BE the church. Truthfully, the mere fact that Jesus declares that we are the church makes me desire to want to be the church even more. In Ephesians 5:27, Jesus epitomizes his relationship with the church to that of a relationship between a husband and wife. He says, "That he might present it to himself a glorious church, not having spot, or wrinkle, or any such thing; but that it should be holy and without blemish."

Before sharing this next part, I want to define precisely what pneumatology is. Pneumatology is the study of the Holy Spirit. To begin the class, we would start by praying in the Spirit, specifically speaking in tongues. As we prayed in the Spirit, I began to sense a connection between myself and the young lady standing in the row ahead of me. After we finished praying, she approached me and admitted that Holy Spirit had been convicting her for not sharing an encouraging word of prophecy with me. She also admitted that God had spoken to her the semester before in one of our previously shared classes. The funny thing was that I had already been asking and seeking God for direction concerning my place of worship. This very moment between this young lady and I was the essential revelation that I needed. Now, I will admit that I didn't fully understand what the young lady meant after she released the word intended for me. However, knowing all too well the power of prayer, she prayed that God would provide confirmation after confirmation of what He was saying. She even took it a step further when she declared six times that a confirmation would come. As the class went on, our instructor took us to Matthew 9:17. This verse says that "Neither do men put new wine into old bottles: else the bottles break, and the wine runneth out, and the bottles perish: but they put new wine into new bottles, and both are preserved." It took a little while before I started to get a sense of what God was telling me. What also seemed to help me was the footnotes section of the Life Application Bible. This is the section where readers of the Bible can get a better understanding and explanation of what a particular Scripture is saying. I can say that because this particular section of the Life Application Bible was an excellent tool for me while studying the Word. It allowed me to see very plainly what God was saying about the Matthew 9:17 Scripture. Not wanting to forget what God made clear to me, I wrote down and dated the prophetic word. The next day, God started to confirm His Word to me. I'd shared it with two mature believers by pointing them to the Scripture in Matthew and the footnotes. Ironically, they both said the same thing, thus confirming what God was prompting me to do. The next day, I received another confirming word that was unsolicited. To sum it all up, I received six confirmations of what I was supposed to do in three days. Three of those confirmations were solicited, and the other three were unsolicited.

Chapter 4

My New Church Family

My time in NBC&S led me to begin my search for my new God-intended church family. This would also be known as a tribe church that taught the word of God and believed wholeheartedly in every word of God. Knowing the proper protocol, I spoke with my current pastor and informed her of what God had said. Without hesitation, she released me and blessed me to go forth in pursuit of my new church. Per our conversation, she understood that I would sometimes be in and out of the service due to visiting other churches. This would go on to be a huge part of discovering where God wanted me to be. I decided that I should first visit Spirit of Faith's newest location in Brandywine, MD. However, I knew that that was going to be a bit of a problem due to not being able to go back and forth to my current church service. Little did I know, I didn't have to worry or be concerned any longer because Holy Spirit reminded me of an 8:00 a.m. service at Victory Christian Ministries International. This would allow me to get back to my then-church's 11:00 a.m. service, which was beneficial because that was the same day that something special was being done for my pastor. What I wasn't prepared for, however, was just how incredible the message at VCMI would be and how it would completely resonate with me. Pastor Tony, one of the pastors of VCMI, taught that day. It was line upon line, precept upon precept, here a little, there a little. The message caused my baby (my spirit) in my womb to leap. By the service's end, an altar call was given. This was, and still is, the part of the service where the churchgoer could give their life to Christ, rededicate their life to Christ, be filled with the Holy Spirit's baptism, or join the church. Sometimes, the churchgoer would do all of the above.

Before I knew it, I gathered my belongings and made my way to the altar. I was shocked at myself because I had no intentions of joining the first church I visited.

I intended to visit a few different houses of worship. However, in the end, God's plan prevailed. In fact, the way God placed me at VCMI reminds me of a particular Scripture. Psalm 37:23 says that "The steps of a good man are ordered by the Lord." With that being said, I could definitely say that God ordered my steps that day. As soon as church concluded at VCMI, I headed to my former church for the special service. For the entire month of June, I attended the 8:00 a.m. service at VCMI and the 11:00 a.m. service at my former church. Every Sunday, Pastor Tony would say, "When God delivers you out of something, don't go back." As a matter of fact, he would close out each service with this statement. Finally, I informed my former pastor of my decision to become a member of VCMI. I knew that I would have to lay my duties of being a Young Adult Ministry leader and Lay Speaker, among other duties, to rest for good. But the more I thought about it, the better I felt, simply because of the commitment I made to follow God and His plan for my life. In addition, it was clear that God wanted me in a place where I could grow, be around other people of like mind and precious faith, and be mentored. With everything happening the way it was happening, I ended up remembering the last statement in the prophetic word I'd received. This statement was that "this decision would change your life and [that] it will be the best one ever."

In November of that year, I got the opportunity to testify of how I'd come to Victory. Within that same moment, there was a stamp of the above statement. In other words, VCMI had certainly changed my life for the better. Specifically, I was no longer searching for more of God in different places due to being hungry. What do I mean by that? Well, consider a light lunch. Now, consider a five-course meal. That's exactly what I think of when I think about VCMI compared to my former church. At my former church, I literally felt like I'd drank water and eaten an appetizer, bread, and salad. In other words, I'd eat everything but the entrée, which would be the most important course of the meal. I would also feel as though I'd have to stop at a couple of different places before I was truly satisfied and full. But when I joined VCMI, this stopped being the case as I no longer left church hungry. On the contrary, I was completely satisfied as I had received prayer, praise and worship, the Word, and fellowship. Just those five spiritual food groups were more than enough to make for a great experience with my Heavenly Father. After all, I knew that God was about relationship and fellowship, not just church as usual, rituals, or religion.

Chapter 5

Back To The Relationship

I want to circle back around to the relationship that I pursued and spoke into existence. I was 18 years old when I got into this relationship. It was my very first one. Don't get me wrong; I liked other guys. I even talked to them on the phone. However, this particular relationship was full-fledged. So, as I stated earlier, he enrolled in the military to establish a future for us. The downside to this was that I'd never been away from my family, and I had no desire to leave them. On top of that, I was just beginning my own life by getting employed in the cosmetology industry, my dream career field. He served a total of three years in the Armed Forces, and he never stopped hoping that I would eventually join him. When that didn't happen, he decided to leave the military and return home in 1988. Unbeknownst to me, he had been cheating on me while he was away. Upon returning home, we began the cycle of breaking up and getting back together. At some point, my size became an issue for him once again. As a result of this, I ended up succumbing to the wiles of another in 1989.

Unfortunately, at this particular time, I was doing the same thing that I didn't want to be done to me due to my low self-esteem and feeling neglected by him. With the other guy, the fling lasted about two to four months before I stopped entertaining him, knowing that I had no real care or concern for him. Admittedly so, I was only using him as much as he was using me. He gave me the attention and words of affirmation that I wanted from my boyfriend at the time. For a short period after my boyfriend and I broke up, I found myself entertaining other guys, including my now ex-boyfriend here and there. In April, we began seeing one another more frequently. By the time June came around, I had discovered that I was pregnant. After relaying the news to my now "former" ex-boyfriend, I found myself between a rock and a hard place. In other words, the decision dwindled down to either having my baby or letting him decide if he was ready for fatherhood. After much thought and consideration on his part, I experienced my one and only pregnancy and abortion that year. It's amazing because right after that, he made it clear that he wanted us to get back together and get engaged again. He put the ring back on my finger after returning to his place from the Planned Parenthood center. Although our relationship was back to square one, I started asking the questions that I should've been asking from the get-go. But the overall crucial question was this: "Was I truly ready to be a wife to this man for the rest of my life…for better or for worse?"

In the midst of it all, both my desire to please God and my conviction concerning fornication was growing. In other words, it would be quicker for me to resist him rather than for me to consent. Over a two and a half year period, I would begin the cycle of breaking up and getting back together…again. During that time, I sought after God and continuously asked Him what I should do.

It's no surprise that this kind of situation would prove to be a bit much (to say the least) for both of us. I could go ahead and credit that to our similar mildly turbulent family lives. In other words, we both suffered severe daddy and family issues. To be specific, he and I were both raised by single moms. Regarding my dad, I know that I lost him when I was five years old. Sadly, he had drowned in the Potomac River. As for my boyfriend's dad, he walked out on him and his mom when he was only 18 months old. Thankfully, I'd found some solace and freedom in my relationship and walk with Christ. I also wasn't ashamed nor afraid to share my life story. On the other hand, my boyfriend insisted that I not share any of his business, which I thought was kind of funny because it was *our* business. Besides, it wasn't like I was sharing our business to gossip or be malicious; it was to get the counsel I needed. I always told him, "I wasn't going to go crazy for him or anyone else by holding things in."

Thanksgiving of 1996 would end up being the finale of our relationship. But in saying that, I'm getting just a little ahead of myself, so let's rewind to the summertime. In June, we got back together again, and he gave me a new engagement ring. However, the question remained of whether or not God had called me to be joined to this man for the rest of my life. In the Young Adult Ministry at our church, he initiated the feeding of the homeless program on Freedom Plaza in D.C. It was such an enjoyable experience, and I honestly wish I could do it again, considering that I find great pleasure in giving. That evening, we returned to my house after a day of serving and having dinner with my family. Unfortunately, his car wasn't working, and I was too tired to drive him home. So, of course, he stayed the night. It was no surprise that he wanted to be intimate with me, which was exactly what I *didn't* want. He was so upset with my decision to remain abstinent that he asked, "When are we gonna get married then? Because I'm tired of this, or we just need to break up." Since I was the one to initiate our breakups in the past, I was excited that he initiated it this time. And on top of that, I was tired of hurting him and putting him on this roller coaster ride of a relationship. When he suggested the parting of ways, I took him up on it. After he said this, he really didn't mean it. However, I was determined to stay the course this time with this decision.

On December 8th of that same year, I visited a friend's church at 8:00 a.m. When the time came, I left that service and went to another friend's church for the 11:00 a.m. service. Before leaving the 8:00 a.m. service, I spoke with my friend and one of his friends that I had previously met. As I was leaving the 11:00 a.m. service, the pastor spoke to me and inquired about what I wanted to ask him. I told him that I didn't need to ask him anything. However, Holy Spirit led him to ask further questions. As a result, I ended up inquiring about a marital relationship. At that moment, my assumption was correct because he ended up stating that God already had a relationship waiting for me, but that He wanted me first. Regarding my desires in a relationship, he stated facts that only God would've known of. As a final confirmation, the pastor added that I would meet my future husband in ten days. Of course, in the days leading up to that tenth day, which would've been the 18th, I got more and more excited, and I had a great expectation. The 18th came and I unfortunately didn't have the pleasure of meeting my future husband. But that was quite alright because I ended up receiving a call on December 28th, which was exactly ten days after the 18th. Who would've known that the abovementioned friend from the church I visited would be the one to call me? But it wouldn't be for the reason you think. It just so happened that he called me because the friend who was with him at the service expressed interest in having my phone number. I figured that this could be the beginning of the God-ordained relationship, so I gave him the "okay" to have my number. From the outside looking in, it appeared that our friendship moved fast, which resulted in our relationship being a whirlwind relationship. He ended up surprising me on our first date by saying the same words that the pastor had shared with me through God. So, of course, I thought that this man was the one I had been waiting for.

Let's circle back around to my ex-boyfriend. On Christmas Eve, he gave me a call and explained that he bought me a gift. He then asked when we could get together so that he could give it to me. As a result, we met on the day after Christmas. We went to dinner, exchanged gifts, and journeyed back home. It didn't surprise me one bit that he tried to convince me to give our relationship another try. It's a good thing I was prepared for that possibility because it resulted in me putting my foot down. Specifically, I had no problem making it clear that we needed to take this time apart and move forward. At the same time, I also concluded that if God's plan was for us to be together, He would reunite us in His time. Just two days later, I began communicating with the other gentleman that I had met. Of course (and unfortunately), my ex-boyfriend continued to try and contact me in more ways than one. He came to my job with the sole purpose of getting me back. A little while later, he would start to become slightly manipulative by mentioning promises that would turn out to be untrue. Prime example, he stated that he would leave me be if I became involved with someone else. Something in me knew that that wasn't true. How did I know that? Well, the minute I broke the news to him, he practically started spiraling out of control.

On Monday, January 27th of 1997, he contacted me and stated that he was leaving town simply because he couldn't handle the fact that we were no longer together. He inquired about what to do with our old pictures and letters. I suggested that he mail them to me. On the next day, I woke up at precisely 8:00 a.m. and began reading my Bible. At the same time, Sherman, my uncle, had just arrived home, as he was living with me at the time. We exchanged our usual morning greetings, and he went straight to bed. At exactly 9:00 a.m., I went downstairs to eat a bowl of cereal. As I sat down, I heard a sound at my front door. Wanting to make sure that my door was completely closed, I got up, journeyed to the living room, and took a look out of my bay window. This was kind of like an acquired habit for me, considering that I am all about safety. I went to my door and opened it. There he stood; my ex-boyfriend. I didn't question him as to why he came to my home unannounced, but I figured that he probably didn't want any trouble. He stated that he came to bring the pictures and letters instead of mailing them. Lord knows that I shouldn't have believed him because he followed behind me the minute I journeyed back to the kitchen for breakfast. Without warning…and sporting military fatigues, which gave me a very uneasy feeling, he placed his bag on my dining room table. He then pulled out his duct tape and his gun and took my phone off the hook, allowing it to be busy. For the final terror, he commanded me to get up and get down on the floor and keep my mouth shut if I wanted Uncle Sherman to live. In other words, one peep out of me and he was going to shoot him if he came downstairs.

Although my heart was beating loudly, and I mean LOUDLY, in my ears, I just couldn't ignore the spirit of boldness that came upon me. I stood up and declared for Satan to get out of my house in the name of Jesus. Before I knew it, Uncle Sherman was downstairs, and he instantly became a narrow victim of my ex-boyfriend's gun. Missing my ex-boyfriend's shot, Uncle Sherman moved back down the hallway, thus protecting himself. The second time, however, my ex-boyfriend shot him in the shoulder blade. I'm under the impression that Uncle Sherman is alive and that all he needs is some medical help. On the other hand, my ex-boyfriend instantly changed after he shot him. Specifically, it became pretty clear that Satan left his body, thus leaving him alone. He commanded me to go upstairs to my bedroom. Within minutes, I heard police sirens, all thanks to my nearby neighbors who heard the gunshots. Little did I know, they weren't able to come to my rescue because I couldn't answer the door. I tried to send an SOS signal with my blinds, but they had already left my eye view. The next few minutes felt like absolute Hell because he proceeded to rape and sodomize me. But the traumatizing event didn't end there.

We proceeded to wrap Uncle Sherman in a sheet per his next commands and drag him out onto my stoop. Then, he deadbolted my lock and allowed me to put my phone back on the hook to call for help. As soon as my phone touched its hook, it rang. To my relief, I discovered that the caller was not only concerned but that she was also one of my best friends. She admitted that the week prior, she saw him stalk me at work by riding a bike to my job in the rain and placing a rose on my windshield. She also admitted that she had tried calling me over and over during my traumatizing event. Although the line was always busy, she knew that something was very wrong. However, she was not one to give up easily because she finally managed to reach me. But, of course, I had absolutely no time to talk because I had a 9-1-1 call to make. She understood very well, as she contacted my grandmother and stated her concerns. They sent an ambulance for Uncle Sherman, thus taking him away.

Within minutes, we received a call from the police, not knowing that it was actually a hostage negotiator. We inquired about Sherman's status, and she replied that he was taken to Fort Washington Hospital, where he was being tended to, and that he would be okay. We thought he'd be okay, but neither of us knew that he died on the scene. The bullets were hollow heads, which explode in your body and strike every vital organ. My ex-boyfriend claimed that he didn't come to hurt anyone but that all he wanted to do was be with me one more time before taking his own life. He held me hostage from 9:00 a.m. until 1:30 p.m. The hostage negotiator and I tried to convince him of reasons not to kill himself. We finally convinced him, and he released me. I got dressed and met the SWAT Team outside. Unsurprisingly, they were ready to take him out. However, he surrendered himself just before they could shoot him. When I was released, I was transported to my other uncle, who was patiently waiting for me down the hill from my home. He informed me that Sherman hadn't survived, which devastated me. I was then transported to Prince George's Hospital for examination.

Following Uncle Sherman's death, my family and I began planning his service. It's funny, and I don't mean funny "ha-ha," I mean funny "peculiar." At a moment like this, I should've been completely heartbroken. Angry. Furious. Sad. Depressed. But I just...wasn't. If anything, I found solace in a couple of things. Firstly, I witnessed to Sherman about giving his life to Christ and returning back to church, which he did. Secondly, he went on to lead Bible Study on Monday nights. In the middle of his class, the question about being ready to transition from earth to eternal life was posed. The last thing he stated was that he was prepared to go "home" and that he wasn't scared. Thirdly, when I viewed Uncle Sherman's body on the day of his service, I noticed that he had a smile on his face. At that moment, I began to praise God and give thanks to Him, as I had never seen that look on someone before. I had peace that it was well with him. In fact, I could easily see that it was and *is* well with him, especially since the Scripture says in 2 Corinthians 5:6, "Therefore we are always confident, knowing that, whilst we are at home in the body, we are absent from the Lord!" Remaining at peace, I began my journey of forgiving my assailant. Speaking of whom, he was charged with first-degree murder, rape, sodomy, gun charge, and holding me hostage. We spoke to the Prosecuting Attorney on his behalf and inquired if they would reduce the charges to second-degree charges simply because first-degree charges carried the death penalty. The agreement was that he would take the plea for the second-degree charges in order to forego a trial. I forgave him because I knew that that's what the Word says for us to do. I also forgave him for my sanity. Matthew 6:12 says, "And forgive us our debts, as we forgive our debtors." Not only was that what I wanted, but I also knew that he allowed the enemy to convince him to do this heinous act of violence without realizing the consequences of his actions.

Chapter 6

God is a Keeper

My Father God has blessed and kept me over these last 20 and counting years. He has freed me of this terrible and painful incident. He allowed me to intercede on my ex-boyfriend's behalf, and He allowed me to want to see the very best for him take place. I was even brave enough to visit him a couple of times before deciding to cut all ties with him. Don't get me wrong; I still pray for the will of God to be done in his life. But nevertheless, I am free, I am whole, and I am delivered. Just as freely as I have received my peace and joy, I just as freely give it away unto others. In other words, I encourage others to know that they can overcome and make it through anything. I assure them that God would provide them beauty for ashes and joy for pain. I assure others that God will keep their minds in perfect peace as long as their minds stay on Him. I help them realize that Father God is always with them through the good and bad, and ups and downs! He's really a trustworthy and comforting God.

Circling back around to the other guy, we continued dating. Truth be told, we were going pretty strong. However, when I went on our church retreat on March 8th of that same year, I was convicted again about not being abstinent. I worked up the courage to let him know what my decision was and thankfully, he was okay with it. However, it wasn't until May that our strong relationship became weak. In other words, I started to notice his change towards me. Not being willing to take any more heartache, I walked away from the relationship. That was actually a great idea because it gave me the courage to walk with the Lord regarding my abstinence. I know for a fact that God has a man for me, and I know that he's a man after His own heart. I also know that we'll walk together fulfilling His purpose and plan for our lives and marriage.

I can't completely express the joy I have for my relationship with my Heavenly Father. In my walk with God, I've discovered that He has called me to teach, preach, proclaim, declare, and live out the Word. Doing what God has me to do will allow me to see my sphere of influence changed, impacted, and on fire for the Kingdom of God. I've received so many prophetic words about my life and how God will use me for His glory to cause multitudes to be healed, delivered, and set free.

One day in 2015, I had this dream about Satan coming for my glory, the same glory that God had given me. In this dream, Pastor Cynthia Brazelton, the other pastor of VCMI, an Elder from my church, some other ladies, and I were at a mansion that we'd rented out to have a fashion show. Everyone had left except the ladies I mentioned above. Being the last one there, I cleaned up and put everything back. I was traveling by motorcycle, so I went out and started its engine. I came back in and concluded my tidying. Suddenly, something led me to open the back door and look around. When I did, I noticed an oriental man standing at the corner of the building. I quickly closed the door and locked it. The next thing I knew, he came to the window, which prompted me to ask him what he wanted. Being honest, he admitted that he came for my glory. He then proceeded to break the window in an attempt to get in. I then fought him with the only thing I had, which was a pencil. I stabbed and punctured him in his neck and throat, allowing myself to have the upper hand. Needless to say, there was NO WAY he was getting my glory! I believe this dream had to do with me needing to write my story and proclaim God's glory. It was pretty evident that in the spiritual realm, the enemy was trying to stop and inhibit me from writing it. Revelation 12:5 says, "And they overcame him by the blood of the Lamb, and by the word of their testimony; and they loved not their lives unto the death." Satan didn't want me to share or write my story, BUT TOO BAD!! IT IS HERE, AND IT IS ETCHED OUT IN PEN AND PAPER!!

Chapter 7

My Resolve

The title of my book, "GOD'S WORD WORKS, NO MATTER HOW U WORK IT!" is a testament to the power of the spoken word(s) that you speak. Whether or not you are aware and/or familiar with the Scriptures, they are words spoken by God through many vessels. These words would go on to reveal to us His heart, will, and intentions for humankind. The Scriptures explain the blessings and benefits of knowing Him intimately, having a relationship with Him, and, like Him, having whatsoever you say. God's word is Life and Spirit, according to John 6:63. Galatians 6:9-10 says, "Let us not lose heart in doing good, for in due time we will reap if we do not grow weary. So then, while we have opportunity, let us do good to all people, and especially to those who are of the household of the faith." Our words are seeds planted in the earth that will take root, spring up, and grow. They will end up producing either a good or bad harvest. My prayer for you, dear reader, is that you become cognizant of your words' power and authority and watch them carefully. Only declare and speak what you really want to have and experience in your life. Genesis 1:3 says, "And God said, Let there be light: and there was light." Just like God did it, we end up creating our worlds by the words we speak.

Right now, I speak a blessing over you in the name of Jesus. I declare that God has encountered you, convicted you, and drawn you closer to Him after reading my story. I pray that you are stirred to watch your words and that you experience the goodness of God despite opposition, test, and trials. He didn't say we wouldn't have trials or bad days. Instead, He said in Psalm 34:19 that "Many are the afflictions of the righteous: but the LORD delivereth him out of them all." This is what you can count on. Trust me; I've been walking it out.

Made in the USA
Middletown, DE
14 October 2021

49706612R00018